BAPTISM

Sacrament of Salvation and Unity

BAPTISM

Sacrament of Salvation and Unity

Titus Babu

2013

BAPTISM: SACRAMENT OF SALVATION AND UNITY–
Published by the Revd Dr Ashish Amos of the Indian Society for Promoting Christian Knowledge (ISPCK), Post Box 1585, 1654 Madarsa Road, Kashmere Gate, Delhi-110006.

© Author, 2013

ISBN : 978-81-8465-310-6

Laser typeset by
ISPCK, Post Box 1585, 1654, Madarsa Road, Kashmere Gate, Delhi-110006.
Tel: 23866322/23
e-mail: *ashish@ispck.org.in* • *ella@ispck.org.in*
website: *www.ispck.org.in*

Dedicated
to all Evangelists working for the glory of God

Contents

Foreword

Many have written books on subjects such as baptism, Jesus Christ and salvation. This book does not deal with doctrines or reflections, but addresses issues concerning baptism in reference to the Word of God—the Bible. It has been written to clear up misunderstandings about baptism and to do away with the erroneous teachings about baptism given by some of our churches and denominations. I am sure that this catechetical form of explanation would enable both evangelists and believers to understand the sacrament of baptism in a better way and help all denominations to be united in one Jesus, one Church and one Baptism—to put it in the words of St. Paul, "be completely united, with one thought and one purpose" (1 Cor. 1:10). Briefly, this book has been written "so that they may be one just as you and I are one" (John.17:21).

Introduction

Baptism is one of the main aspects of Christian life, and it is through the sacrament of baptism that one is saved from the clutches of sin and death and gets into a union with Christ. It is very much appreciable to know the missionaries involved in evangelisation of the Kingdom of God and making disciples for Christ by fulfilling the will of Jesus: "Go everywhere and make them my disciples by baptizing them" (Matt. 28:19).

Being a missionary, I came across many people who had quite a few queries about baptism. It is rather sad to say that there are many misunderstandings about the administration of baptism; and that is because not many are so sure about what the Bible says about baptism. The various teachings of different denominations have only made matters worse. People are therefore confused and in desperate need for answers.

With the help of the Holy Spirit, I have tried to put down in this booklet the correct teachings about baptism. Answers to all the questions raised in this booklet are based on the Holy Bible. I hope this booklet answers all relevant questions about baptism.

I thank all those who have helped me to bring out this booklet. All biblical quotes in this booklet are from *Good News Bible*, published by Society of St. Paul, India.

Fr. Titus Babu

CHAPTER 1

What Is Baptism?

This chapter deals with the scriptural description of baptism, the effect of baptism on the receiver, condition for receiving baptism and ways of receiving and administering baptism.

What is baptism?

In Romans 6:3-6, St. Paul writes: "Do you not know that all of us who have been baptized into Christ Jesus were baptized into his death? Therefore we have been buried with him by baptism into death, so that just as Christ was raised from the dead by the glory of the Father" (v 4). The reference to being "buried into death by baptism" refers to the spiritual rebirth that baptism gives. It puts to death the man who lives in the Original Sin (sin by first parents) and gives birth to a new man in Christ.

The English word "baptise" is derived from the Greek *baptizo*, which means to "plunge" or "immerse." According to the Bible, it means "to bury beneath the water", symbolising the candidate's burial into Christ's death from which he or she rises up by resurrection with him as a "new creature" (2 Cor. 5:17; Gal. 6:15; Rom. 6:3-4; Col. 2:12). So, the real meaning of baptism is "immersion", a total immersion in faith in Jesus. In other words, it means dying in Jesus and rising with Jesus in faith and being cleansed of the Original Sin.

Baptism can also be described as a sacrament instituted by Christ through which one is initiated into Christianity by the cleansing of the Original Sin; one becomes the child of the Heavenly Father, the heir to Heaven; one becomes worthy of receiving the Holy Spirit and Grace. We become brothers and sisters in Jesus Christ through baptism (Catechism of the Catholic Church, No. 1213).

"Go, then to all peoples everywhere and make them my disciples; baptize them in the name of the Father, the Son, and the Holy Spirit" (Matt. 28:19). Baptism is making one a disciple of Jesus.

Why do we need to receive baptism? How does baptism become effective in a person?

By his sacrificial death we are now put right with God (Rom. 5:9). The Salvation Army and the Quakers say since Jesus died once and for all there is no more sin and all are saved for eternity; therefore, baptism is not needed. It is objectively true that Jesus brought salvation to all humankind from the beginning of the first promise of God the Father after the first sin of the first parents to the Second Coming of Jesus. But it becomes subjectively effective only when one believes in Jesus and accepts baptism. For example, the mother prepares food and serves it but if one does not eat it, one's hunger remains unsatisfied. Consider another example. Let us say, we have a school in our neighbourhood, but if we do not go to it, we would neither receive the education it provides nor the certificate it awards. Therefore, subjective participative reception of salvation is very important.

What are the conditions and requirements for baptism?

The requirements for receiving baptism are as follows:

- Having faith
- Being repentant
- Turning away from sins

- Obeying the commandments of God

According to Matthew 28:19-20 and Mark 16:16, one needs to have faith in Jesus and his Gospel to receive true baptism. Look at Acts 8:34-37: "And the eunuch answered Philip, and said..., what is to keep me from being baptized? And Philip said, 'You may be baptized if you believe with all your heart.' 'I do', he answered; 'I believe that Jesus Christ is the Son of God.'"

"Then Peter said unto them, Repent, and be baptized every one of you in the name of Jesus Christ for the remission of sins, and you shall receive the gift of the Holy Ghost" (Acts 2:38).

"Go then to all peoples everywhere and make them my disciples; baptize them in the name of the Father, the Son, and the Holy Spirit, and teach them to obey everything I have commanded you" (Matt. 28:19-20).

Besides the recipient should be properly initiated into the mystery of salvation, practice of evangelical virtues and introduced to the life of faith, liturgy and charity of the people of God by successive sacred rites (Catechism of Catholic Church, 1230, p. 244).

How does one receive the sacrament of baptism?

The baptism is received in the 'name', which means in the name of Heavenly Father, His Son and the Holy Spirit. The following passages tell us that Jesus asked his disciples to do so:

"Go therefore and make disciples of all nations, baptizing them in the name of the Father and of the Son and of the Holy Spirit, and teaching them to obey everything that I have commanded you" (Matt. 28:19-20).

"The one who believes and is baptized will be saved; but the one who does not believe will be condemned" (Mark 16:16). Here we need to note that Jesus never asks us to get immersed in the water but to baptise in the 'name'.

"Let me put it this way; each one of you say something different. One says 'I follow Paul; another 'I follow Apollos'; another 'I follow Christ.' Christ has been divided into groups! Was it Paul who died on the cross for you? Where you baptized as Paul's disciples?" (1 Cor. 1:12, 13, 15) "No one can say then that you were baptized as my disciples" (v. 15).

Is the Trinitarian form or only the name of Jesus enough for baptism?

Baptising in the Trinitarian form was the command of Jesus (Matt. 28:19) and was practiced in the early Church. However, the Bible tells us that baptising only in the name of Jesus was also prevalent. So, both were prevalent.

"While Peter was speaking the Holy Spirit came down on all those who were listening to his message" (Acts 2:38, 10:44-48). "So he ordered them to be baptized in the name of Jesus Christ" (v.48).

"They were baptized in the name of the Lord Jesus" (Acts 19:1-5). Here we must understand that the name of Jesus includes (John 14:10) all three persons of Trinity. This does not mean that we should not use the Trinitarian form, rather it is the command of Jesus to use the Trinitarian form as well, asking his disciples to baptise the believer in the name of the Father, the Spirit and his own name (Matt. 28.18-19). Therefore, the Trinitarian form is compulsory and is an accepted form and common form of baptism.

What does the Bible say about one baptism?

The Bible says that all true believers have received one baptism; therefore, one comes into the Body of Christ (the Church) and receives the Holy Spirit through baptism.

In Ephesians 4:1-6, St. Paul describes the unity in the Church of Jesus Christ. Consider the list he gives: "One Lord, one faith, one baptism; there is one God and Father of all mankind, who is Lord of all, works through all, and is in all." This is because it is through this baptism that one becomes united to God and to the Church. To say that people in the Church do not have this baptism is equivalent to saying that they do not have one Lord and one faith.

"Careful to keep the unity of the Spirit in the bond of peace. One body and one Spirit; as you are called in the hope of your calling. One Lord, one faith, one baptism, One God and Father of all…" (Eph. 4:4-6).

1 Corinthians, chapter 12, teaches that baptism makes one a member of the body of Christ. "For by one Spirit are we all baptized into one body, whether we be Jews or Gentiles, whether we be bond or free" (v.13).

Baptism is the first and chief sacrament of forgiveness of sins because it unites us with Christ, who died for our sins and rose for our justification, so that "we too might walk in newness of life" (Rom. 6:4, 4:25).

CHAPTER 2

Baptism and Sin

This chapter deals with aspects of Sin (original and personal) and how sins are forgiven through baptism and repentance (reconciliation), leading the baptised to salvation.

What is sin?

Sin is disobedience to God. It is an aversion from God, (A New Catechism Catholic Faith for Adults by Herder and Herder, N.Y., 1969). According to Romans 5:1, 19, "Sin came into the world through one man, and his sin brought death with it. As a result, death has spread to the whole human race because everyone has sinned (v.19). Just as all people were made sinners as the result of the disobedience of one man, in the same way they will all be put right with God as the result of the obedience of the one man." And the Psalmist says in Psalms 50:51: "Oh see in guilt I was born, a sinner I was conceived."

Does baptism remove the Original Sin?

Yes. St. Paul explains in Romans chapters 5 and 6 that through baptism Christ reconciles men to God, removes their Original Sin (affected by the sin of Adam and Eve) and makes them members of God's family.

Why are we in sin again, even after the reception of the Sacrament of Baptism?

The Sacrament of Baptism removes all sins (sins of first parents and actual sins) for those who properly receive it. It should be noted, however, that receiving the sacrament is not a guarantee of salvation. One can lose the grace of baptism through mortal sins and by denying true faith in Jesus Christ. In John 8:34, 35, Jesus said, "Everyone who sins is a slave of Sin. A slave does not belong to family permanently" (v.35). Here the sins are in plural; these are the sins due to the effect of the first sin. It is like the amoebas in our body; even if we get rid of them through antibiotics or medicine, the effect remains; or it is like the Tuberculoses patient's children—even after the patient gets well, the effect is passed on to the patient's children. Even though Jesus brought salvation to humankind, the stain of sin remains—the scar remains even after the wound has been healed; the stain of sin is passed on to future generations even after the reception of baptism.

How are sins committed (personal sins) after baptism forgiven?

The grace of baptism delivers no one from all weaknesses of nature. On the contrary, we must continue to combat concupiscence, which can lead us into evil. Therefore, Jesus himself instituted the holy Sacrament of Confession. "Jesus said to them again, 'Peace be with you. As the Father has sent me, so I send you.' When he had said this, he breathed on them and said to them 'Receive the Holy Spirit. If you forgive the sins of any they are forgiven them; if you retain the sins of any, they are retained'" (John 20:19-23). It may be noted that 'sin' is addressed here as sins—in plural. So sins committed after baptism are forgiven through the Sacrament of Confession or Reconciliation. One receives peace through the sacrament of reconciliation; and the Apostles and their successors carry out this ministry of reconciliation not only by announcing to men God's forgiveness merited for us by Christ and calling them to conversion and faith, but also by communicating to them the forgiveness of sins in baptism and reconciling them with God and the Church through the power of the keys received from Christ (Catechism of Catholic Church.1444). Through this Sacrament of Penance, the baptised can be reconciled with God and the Church. Penance has rightly been called by the holy Fathers "a laborious kind of baptism." This Sacrament of Penance is necessary for salvation for those who have fallen after baptism, just as baptism is necessary for salvation for those who have not yet been reborn (Catechism of Catholic church.1422).

"Should we continue in sin in order that grace may abound? By no means! How can we who died to sin go on living in it?" (Rom. 6:1-2). "All this is from God, who reconciled us to himself through Christ, and has given us the ministry of reconciliation(2 Cor. 5:18), that is in Christ God was reconciling the world to himself, not counting their trespasses against them, and entrusting the message of reconciliation to us" (v.19). We know that Christ, being raised from the dead, will never die again; death no longer has dominion over him (v.9). So you also must consider yourselves dead to sin and alive to God in Christ Jesus (v.11). For sin will have no dominion over you, since you are not under law but under grace" (Rom. 6:9-14).

How can I justify that Jesus died for me 2,000 years ago whereas I live now?

Of course, Jesus died 2000 years ago to free me from the stain of the Original Sin (first sin) committed by the first parents, Adam and Eve, by their disobedience; as a result, the punishment and mortality affected all humanity. The effects of the first parents' sin continue to exist even now and even after the salvific action of Jesus Christ.

I believe Jesus died for me and for all humanity of all time to save us from the stain of the Original Sin found in every one born of flesh and blood. This is possible only by believing in Jesus as my personal saviour who died for me and rose from the dead, accepting him, receiving baptism in his name and taking part subjectively in his redemptive action.

CHAPTER 3

Effect and Grace
of Baptism

I n this chapter, we will look at the effects and graces received through baptism. What did the Fathers of the Church teach us about the effects and grace of baptism?

What are the graces, relation and privileges that follow the recipient of baptism?

The Original Sin is cleansed: We receive the sanctifying grace by the cleansing of the Original Sin and personal sins and all the punishment for sin (Rom. 5:12). In those who have been reborn, nothing remains that would impede their entry into the kingdom of God (Catechism of Catholic Church.977). In Acts 2:38-39, St. Peter says,

"Your sins will be forgiven; and you will receive God's gift, the Holy Spirit (v.39) for God's promise was made to you and your children."

Receive the Holy Spirit: As soon as Jesus came up out of the water, he saw heaven opening and the Spirit coming down on him like a dove. And a voice came from heaven: "You are my own dear son, I am pleased with you" (Mark.1:10-11). In Acts 1:4, 5, Jesus says, "John baptized with water, but in a few days you will be baptized with the Holy Spirit." "Suddenly there was a noise from the sky which sounded like a strong wind blowing, and it filled the whole house where they were sitting. Then they saw what looked like tongues of fire which spread out and touched each person there. They were all filled with the Holy Spirit and began to talk in other languages as the Spirit enabled them to speak (Acts 2:2-4, 14). The Spirit led them to speak" (v.14).

Become one and union with Christ: In Romans 6:3-5, we read: "When we were baptized into union with Christ Jesus, we were baptized into union with his death. By our baptism, then we were buried with him and shared his death, in order that, just as Christ was raised from death by the glorious power of the Father, so also we might live a new life (v.4). For since we have become one with him in dying as he did, in the same way we shall be one with him by being raised to life as he was(v.5). And we know that our old being has been put to death with Christ on his cross, in order that the power of the sinful self might be destroyed, so that we should no longer be the slaves of sin" (v.6). In Romans 6:12, we see "alive in union with Christ" and in Ephesians 4:25 "Everyone must tell the truth to his fellow-believer, because we are all members together in the body of Christ."   Galatians 3:27 reads "For as many of you as have been baptized in Christ, have put on Christ. There is neither Jew nor Greek: there is neither bond nor free: there is neither male nor female. For you are all one in Christ Jesus." St. Paul explains exactly what he means by "faith in Christ Jesus"—fullness of life in Christ dying and living with Christ. The old life and the new life (Col. 2:6-3:17).

Become members of the Church: In Ephesians 2:18-22, St. Paul says, "To come in the one Spirit into the presence of the Father, you are now fellow-citizens with God's people and members of the family of God." 1Peter 2:5-10 reads: "Come as living stone, and let yourselves be used in building the spiritual temple, where you will serve as holy priests to offer spiritual and acceptable sacrifices to God through Jesus Christ" (v.5). "You are the chosen race, the King's priests, the holy nation, God's own people, chosen to proclaim the wonderful acts of God, who called you out of darkness into his marvelous light, and now you have received his mercy" (vs.9-10). 1 Corinthians 12:13 reads: "In the same way all of us have been baptized into the one body by the same Spirit, and we have all been given the one Spirit to drink." "The group of believers was one in mind and heart" (Acts 4:32-35).

Having become a member of the Church, the baptised person is no longer to himself but to him who died and rose for us (1 Cor. 6:19; 2 Cor. 5:15). From now on he is called to be subject to others to serve them in the communion of the Church, and obey and submit to the Church's leaders holding them in respect and affection (Heb.13:17-18).

Receive God's graces: Romans 15:8 reads: "For I tell you that Christ has become a servant of the circumcised on behalf of the truth of God in order that he might confirm the promises given to the Patriarchs." In Mark 16.15-18, Jesus said to them, "Go throughout the whole world and preach the gospel to all mankind. Whoever believes and is baptized will be saved; whoever does not believe will be condemned. Believers will be given the power to perform miracles: they will speak in strange tongues; if they pick up snakes or drink any poison, they will not be harmed; they will place their hands on sick people, who will get well." "You will be filled with power and you will be witness for me" (Acts 1:8).

In short, it is called gift because it is conferred on those who bring nothing of their own grace since it is given even to the guilty; baptism because sin is buried in the water, anointing for it is priestly and royal as are those who are anointed; enlightenment because it radiates light (Matt. 8:12: "I am the light of the world, whoever follows me will have the light of life and will never walk in darkness." Matt. 5:14: "You are the light of the world." Col. 1:12-13); clothing because it veils our shame (Gal. 3:27); you were Baptized into union with Christ, and now you are clothed); bathing symbolises washing away of sins (1 Cor. 6:11, 12:13; Eph. 5:26); and seal because it is our guard and the sign of God's lordship (Catechism of Catholic Church 1243).

What is meant by baptismal regeneration?

The washing of regeneration and renewal by the Holy Spirit actually brings about the birth of water and the spirit without which no one "can enter the Kingdom of God" (Titus 3:5; John 3:5).

The descent of the Holy Ghost signifies the regenerative powers of baptism. The opening of Heaven signifies that Heaven is opened to a person who has properly received baptism. It makes the person an adopted son or daughter of God, instead of a fallen child of Adam. According to Luke 3:21-22, "It came to pass, that Jesus also being baptized, and praying, the heaven was opened, and the Holy Ghost descended in a bodily shape like a dove upon him, and a voice came from heaven, which said, 'Thou art my beloved Son; in thee I am well pleased.'"

But most of the denominations today do not believe that baptism regenerates. This includes Baptists, Presbyterians, Pentecostals, most Evangelicals and many others. They do not believe that baptism removes sin from the soul and places man in a state of justification. Their position is that water baptism should be performed as just a sign of initiation, a sign of a conversion from personal sins or a spiritual rebirth that has already happened.

What did the Fathers of the Church teach about baptismal regeneration?

From the very beginning of the Church, the Fathers of the Church unanimously believed in the necessity of water baptism and baptismal regeneration. They based their belief on the teaching of the New Testament, John 3:5

and the Apostolic Tradition. Given below are just four passages. One could quote dozens of other passages.

1. In the Letter of Barnabas, dated as early as 70 A.D., we read: "... we descend into the water full of sins and foulness, and we come up bearing fruit in our heart..." (Jurgens, *The Faith of the Early Fathers*, vol. 1:34.)

2. In the Shepherd of Hermas, dated 140 A.D., Hermas quotes Jesus in John 3:5 and writes: "They had needed to come up through the water, so that they might be made alive; for they could not otherwise enter into the kingdom of God" (Jurgens, *The Faith of the Early Fathers*, Vol. 1:92).

3. In 155 A.D., in First Apology, 61, St. Justin the Martyr writes: "... they are led by us to a place where there is water; and there they are reborn in the same kind of rebirth in which we ourselves were reborn... in the name of God... they receive the washing of water. For Christ said, 'Unless you be reborn, you shall not enter into the kingdom of heaven.' The reason for doing this we have learned from the apostles" (Jurgens, *The Faith of the Early Fathers*, Vol. 1:126).

4. St. Aphraates, the oldest of the Syrian Fathers, writes
   in his *Treatises*, 336 A.D.:"For from baptism we receive
   the Spirit of Christ… For the Spirit is absent from
   all those who are born of the flesh, until they come
   to the water of re-birth" (Jurgens, *The Faith of the
   Early Fathers*, Vol. 1: 681).

The Catholic position is that baptism is necessary for
salvation. The Catholic Church teaches that baptism is
necessary for every man because baptism is the cause of
spiritual rebirth. Baptism regenerates. Acts 2:37-38 reads:
"But Peter said to them: Do penance, and be baptized
every one of you in the name of Jesus Christ, for the
remission of your sins: and you shall receive the gift of
the Holy Ghost." "And one Ananias… came unto me,
and stood, and said unto me, 'Brother Saul, receive thy
sight. And the same hour I looked up upon him. And [he
said] '… arise, and be baptized, and wash away thy sins,
calling on the name of the Lord'" (Acts 22:12-16).

Do we receive faith through baptism?

In Galatians 3:23-27, we see the link between receiving
faith and receiving baptism; especially one first receives
faith through baptism.

In verse 23, St. Paul says: "But before, the faith
came … ."

In verse 24, he says: "That we may be justified by faith... ."

In verse 25, he says: "But after the faith is come... .""

In verse 26, he says: "For you are all the children of God by faith, in Christ Jesus."

Mark 9:24 "I do have faith, but not enough. Help me to have more." It ultimately points to the fact that faith is something that one is given, not something that one produces oneself (A New Catechism, Catholic Faith for Adults, by Herder, N.Y, 1969).

These interesting chapters of Scripture should give a message to everyone. It is clearly teaching what the Catholic Church has held for 2,000 years: It is by means of the Sacrament of Baptism that one is strengthened in faith. That's why baptism has been, since Apostolic times, called "the Sacrament of faith." Without baptism, one does not have the faith and cannot be saved.

CHAPTER 4

Baptism and Water

T his chapter covers the importance and significance of water in administering baptism.

Is water necessary for baptism or salvation?

Yes. Baptism by water is necessary for salvation. In John 3:5, Jesus says, "Truly, I say unto thee, except a man be born of water and of the Spirit, he cannot enter into the kingdom of God."

It is crucial for people to understand that John 3:5 refers to water baptism; for millions have a false and unbiblical concept of what it means to be born again. They think that it means coming to a true commitment, that Jesus is the Saviour. It is certainly necessary for a person above the age of reason to accept Jesus Christ, to believe in the Trinity and the Incarnation and to accept all his teachings. But the Bible clearly teaches that being born again refers to the spiritual regeneration that baptism of water brings. The overwhelming evidence that we have considered from other passages in the Bible also proves it.

Genesis 1:1-2 says: "In the beginning God created the heaven and the earth. And the earth was without form, and void; and darkness was upon the face of the deep. And the Spirit of God moved upon the face of the waters." This tells us that water has been of major and even unique significance to God's creation from the very beginning. It has been integral to His plan. He has used it to cleanse, to generate new life. It makes perfect sense, therefore, that the element He would choose in bringing the new life of Jesus Christ to souls by dispensing the merit of His passion, death and resurrection and the cleansing of the Holy Spirit is that primordial element over which His Spirit moved at the beginning of creation.

Another reference to the sanctifying effects of water baptism is found in Ezekiel 36:24-26: "For I will take you from among the heathen, and gather you out of all countries, and will bring you into your own land. Then will I sprinkle clean water upon you, and you shall be clean: from all your filthiness, and from all your idols, will

I cleanse you. A new heart also will I give you, and a new spirit will I put within you." This clearly refers to the cleansing power of water baptism, which will transmit the new life of Jesus Christ and will be dispensed to God's people gathered from all over the earth. The reference to "clean water" in Ezekiel 36:25 proves that it is referring to justification in the New Testament; for the very same language is found in Heb.10:22, 36 to describe the interior change effectuated by justification in Christ. Verse 36 specifically indicates that this cleanness of heart is effectuated by the sprinkling with clean water (in baptism). Besides, for the ritual fulfillment of washing of the sins water is used. We see in Leviticus 11:15 that the Jews were familiar with ritual washing. William Barclay, in his book *The Daily Study Bible* (p.13), says, "The Jew washes himself every day because every day he is defiled", so symbolic washing and purifying were woven into the very fabric of Jewish ritual.

Does water remove sin?

Of course, water cannot wash sins, if so no sin could be found in those who bath everyday. According to 1 Peter 3:20-21, "The eight people in Noah's boat were saved by the water, which was a symbol pointing to baptism, which now saves you. It is not washing away of bodily dirt, but the promise made to God from a good conscience. It saves you through the resurrection of Jesus Christ." Therefore, it is repentance, true intention and faith in the name of the true God that cleanses us from the Original Sin. Just like water washes bodily dirt so also baptism cleanses the soul from sin or spiritual illness. Water does not give salvation but, as John the Baptist says, it is the Holy Spirit who does.

"He will baptize with the Holy Spirit" (Mark 1:8; John 1:33, Acts 2:1-4).

Why do we use water in baptism?

We use water in baptism because, according to scripture, water is holy and has cleansing and saving power. In Genesis 1:2, we find that "the (Spirit) of God was moving over the water"; therefore, water is holy (Isa. 44:3). And in Genesis chapters 6, 7 and 8, the story of Flood and Noah, and Exodus 14:21-25, the Israelites are saved through the sea. In Numbers 19:2-10 (v.9), "they are to be kept for the Israelite community to use in preparing the water for removing ritual un-cleanness. This ritual is performed to remove sin." The Psalmist prays (Psalms 50 (51):7): "Remove my sin, and I will be clean, wash me, and I will be whiter than snow." Also, in Ezekiel 36:25, it is written, "I will sprinkle clean water on you and make you clean."

What does the Bible say about the saying "water baptism saves"?

Titus 3:5 says: "Not by works of righteousness which we have done, but according to his mercy he saved us, by the washing of regeneration, and renewing of the Holy Spirit." So the Bible says that men are saved by the "washing of regeneration and renewing of the Holy Spirit." This refers to the spiritual regeneration given in baptismal waters. The outward pouring of water affects the interior cleansing and renewal by the Holy Spirit. This sacramental action justifies the soul and applies the merit of the blood of Jesus Christ while baptism is occurring.

Some of the denominations have tried to explain Titus 3:5 away. They argue that the "washing" does not refer to the water of baptism, but to the cleansing by the Holy Spirit without baptism. This is refuted by comparing this passage to 1 Peter 3:20-21: "When they waited for the patience of God in the days of Noah, when the ark was a building: wherein a few, that is, eight souls were saved by water. Whereunto baptism being of the like form, now saves you also…" They both teach that baptism "saves." 1 Peter 3:20-21 is clearly referring to water baptism, not just a spiritual washing. This demonstrates that Titus 3:5 is also referring to regeneration through the water of baptism.

Baptism now saves you. Peter is talking about water baptism (the Sacrament), because he draws an analogy between baptismal waters and flood waters. Peter compares receiving the Sacrament of (water) baptism to being on the ark of Noah. Just as no one escaped physical death outside the ark of Noah during the time of the Flood (only eight souls survived the Flood by being firmly planted on the ark), likewise no one avoids spiritual death or is saved from the Original Sin without baptism.

Another example is from Ephesians 5:25-26: "Husbands, love your wives, even as Christ also loved the church, and gave himself for it; that he might sanctify it, cleansing it by the laver of water in the word of life." The Church is sanctified and cleansed by the laver (or washing) of water in the eternal word of life. What is this washing of water? It obviously refers to water baptism. The "word of life" refers to the words that were given by Jesus for the baptismal form (Matt. 28:19). Even John Calvin, the famous Protestant who denied baptismal regeneration, admitted that this passage (Eph. 5:26) refers to water baptism.

What is meant by "born of water and the Spirit" in reference to John 3:5?

This means Sacramental Baptism. Sacramental Baptism is instituted by Christ Himself. Jesus says, "No one enters heaven without rebirth of water and of the spirit." "Jesus answered, 'I am telling you the truth: no one can see the kingdom of God unless he is born again'" (John 3:3-5). Verse 5 reads: "No one can enter the kingdom of God unless he is born of water and the Spirit. Verse 6 reads: "A person is born physically of human parents, but he is born spiritually of the Spirit." So, being born again means being born of water and the Holy Spirit. This clearly refers to water baptism.

It is true that non-Catholics have tried to explain away the clear meaning of these words, but to no avail. Many of them say that water refers to natural birth and the Spirit refers to the born-again process by accepting the faith. That is impossible because the passage is about rebirth. Jesus says that the rebirth is of water and the Spirit. Moreover, the phrase "of water and the Spirit" in Greek (*ek hudatos kai pneumatos*) is a single linguistic unit, as Greek scholars point out. It describes being "born of water and the Spirit," not "born of water", on the one hand, and "born of the Spirit", on the other. In addition, the extended context of the passage confirms that it refers to water baptism. In the very next chapter, we read that Jesus' Apostles went out and baptised. Look at John 4:1. It mentions that the Apostles practiced what Jesus preached.

Is a river needed to baptise a candidate?

It is not compulsory to have either a river or total physical immersion. What is important is the use of water and proper words. If people are so adamant in having immersion in the river, they should not forget that Jesus never said that all should get baptism in the river of Jordan or in any other river. If we are very particular about the river, then should it not be the river Jordan where Jesus himself had his baptism?

Ananias baptised Saul (Paul) in his house, not in the river (Acts 9:17-19). Acts 22:16 reads: "And now why wait any longer? Arise, and be baptized, and wash away thy sins, calling on the name of the Lord." There is no mention of a river in this verse. Consider another example. In Acts 8:36, "some water" indicates that the Ethiopian was not given baptism in a river.

CHAPTER 5

Baptism and Immersion

Though the word "baptism" means "immersion", it does not mean that Baptism of Immersion is compulsory. The actual meaning is deepening our faith in Jesus and his salvific act and cleansing of sin.

Is Baptism by Immersion compulsory to go to Kingdom of Heaven?

No. What is important for salvation is baptism. What is important is the use of water as a symbol of cleansing, which could be by pouring, by sprinkling or by immersion. In Matthew 3:11, John the Baptist says, "I baptize you with water to show that you have repented, but the one who will come after me will baptize you with the Holy Spirit and fire." So, should we put fire on our body?

Some non-Catholics believe that baptism must be done only by immersion. The Bible does not support this belief. Consider the fact that on Pentecost, in Acts chapter 2, when thousands were baptised, there was not sufficient water supply to baptise them all by immersion. Therefore, baptism by effusion (pouring) or sprinkling must have been used.

In addition, baptism by immersion would be very difficult or impossible in extremely cold environments such as the Arctic and deserts; also, in other situations, such as sickly people and the hospitalised and places where evangelisation and religious freedom are being restricted. Consider the following example: Apostles giving baptism to the jailer and all the others in his house (Acts 16:29-34). Jesus never would have made baptism so difficult or impossible to administer when He was the one who declared that every man must have it.

Some people also say that the word "baptism" in Greek means "immersion". This is not true. The word is used to signify immersion, but it is also used to signify washings that are not immersion. Examples to show that baptism also meant washing but not immersion are found in Luke 11:38 and Hebrew 9:10. Baptism is valid if performed either by immersion, pouring or sprinkling—but the water must be moving as it strikes the body—and proper words: "I baptise you in the name of the Father, the Son and the Holy Spirit."

Besides, in baptism, the Holy Spirit is poured out. This means that even though baptism by immersion is certainly valid if done properly, one can say that baptism by effusion (i.e., pouring) more precisely signifies the action of the Holy Spirit in baptism. There is also the fact that paintings in the catacombs that were made by the earliest Christians depict acts of baptism by pouring. This shows that baptism by pouring was considered acceptable from the beginning.

The Didache was written around A.D. 70. It is a famous document from the early Church. It is a strong witness to the beliefs and practices of the ancient Christians. In chapter 7, *The Didache* approves of baptism by immersion in river, but also baptism by effusion or pouring. "And concerning baptism, thus baptize: Having first said all these things, baptize into the name of the Father, and of the Son, and of the Holy Spirit, in living water. But if you have no living water, baptize into other water; and if you cannot in cold, in warm. But if you have not either, pour out water thrice upon the head in the name of Father and Son and Holy Spirit." This was written while some of the Apostles might have been living or in the first generation after them.

Does the Catholic Church teach against baptism by immersion?

No. The Catholic Church gives freedom to have any form of baptism, but water together with the Trinitarian formula must be used.

The practice of sprinkling or pouring water for baptism crept into the Church during the twelfth century A.D. History preserves this record: "For several centuries after the establishment of Christianity, baptism was usually conferred by immersion; but since the twelfth century, the practice of baptism by infusion (pouring) has prevailed in the Catholic Church, as this manner is attended with less inconvenience than baptism by immersion. The Church exercises her discretion in adapting the most convenient modes, according to the circumstances of time and place" (James Cardinal Gibbons, *Faith of Our Fathers*, p.277).

Did Jesus receive baptism by immersion? Should we also need to follow the same ritual?

We do not have clear proof of Jesus receiving baptism of immersion. According to Mark 1:10, Jesus "straightway coming up out of the water … saw the heavens opened, and the Spirit like a dove descending upon him." Based on this quotation we cannot affirm that Jesus did have baptism of immersion. He may be coming out of the water to the shore too. The following examples give us a clear picture of this: Firstly, let us take a look at the Baptism of Ethiopian by Philip in Acts 8:36-39. "There was some water and the official said, 'Here is some water'" (v.36). Now "some water" makes sure that one cannot get the entire body dipped into the water as one may think about baptism. "Both Philip and the official went down into the water, and Philip baptized him" (v.38). Now, if "both went down into the water", then how can Philip give baptism to the Ethiopian? So, here we must understand that both went into the water but total immersion did not take place. "When they came up out of the water" (v.39) —here also it is clear that after baptism, both came out of water. So, this example gives us the correct picture of the kind of baptism Jesus Christ received.

Secondly, the pictures in the Catacombs show John pouring water on Jesus. Thirdly, we do not follow everything that Jesus did; for example, Jesus followed the custom of circumcision as the sign of covenant. This is a law from God the Father, but we do not follow it. So also in Matthew 3:15, Jesus himself tells at his baptism that this "is to fulfill all righteousness." Jesus had baptism in a river, but this does not mean that we too must have baptism in a river. Jesus never said that one should have baptism of immersion; just getting baptised is what matters. Besides, the purpose of baptism is removal of the Original Sin and not just following mere rituals.

CHAPTER 6

Infant Baptism

Circumcision for infants of the Old Testament was compulsory, and baptism for people of the New Testament is obligatory. Baptism is important because it is the way to eternal life and reception of the Holy Spirit.

What does the Old Testament (the Jewish law) say about circumcision and infant baptism?

According to Leviticus 12:1, "for seven days after a woman gives birth to a son, she is ritually unclean as she is during her monthly period. On the eighth day, the child shall be circumcised" (v.3).

In Genesis 17:9-14, especially in verse 12, it is said that "you must circumcise every baby boy when he is eight days old; including slaves born in your homes, and slaves bought from foreigners. This will show that there is a covenant between you and me. Each one must be circumcised, and this will be a physical sign to show that my covenant with you is everlasting. Any male who has not been circumcised will no longer be considered one of my people, because he has not kept the covenant with me." Therefore, we see in Genesis 21:4, when Isaac was eight days old, Abraham circumcised him as God had commanded.

And in Luke 2:22-24, it is written that "after eight days had passed, it was time to circumcise the child; and he was called Jesus, the name given by the angel before he was conceived in the womb. When the time came for their purification according to the law of Moses, they brought him up to Jerusalem to present him to the Lord (v.22) (as it is written in the Law of the Lord, "every firstborn male shall be designated as holy to the Lord" [v.23]) and they offered a sacrifice according to what is stated in the law of the Lord, "a pair of turtledoves or two young pigeons" (v.24).

Infants were circumcised in the Old Testament, and the Bible teaches that baptism is the new circumcision. If baptism is the new circumcision, it follows that infants are also to be baptised in the New. If not, then God would have been more generous, more universal and more inclusive in the inferior Old Covenant than He is in the

New. But this is not the case. Therefore, in Colossians 2:11, St. Paul says, "In union with Christ you were circumcised not with the circumcision that is made by men, but with the circumcision made by Christ, which consists of being freed from the power of this sinful self."

What do the Apostles say about infant baptism?

The salvation that is made available in Jesus is open to all peoples: Jews and Gentiles. It is unthinkable that Jesus would not establish a means to incorporate children into His spiritual Kingdom and to give them His blessings and salvation. We see a number of proofs in the Bible about infant baptism.

"I (Paul) baptized also the household of Stephanas" (1 Cor. 1:16). Household means that even infants are included. "And when she [Lydia] was baptized, and her household (Acts 16:15); Gentiles receiving baptism (Acts 10:48). The gentiles include all the members. In Caesarea, Cornelius and his whole family were baptised (Acts 11:13-17); "Crispus and all his family in Corinth heard the message, believed, and were baptized" (Acts 18:8); "and he took them the same hour of the night, and washed their stripes; and was baptized, he and all his, straightway" (Acts 16:33).

Entire households were baptised. The Bible refers to a woman and "her household." It refers to a man and his "household." Why didn't the passage just say a woman and "her husband"? Why didn't it say a man and "his wife"? The household baptised generally includes children too. There is nothing in the Bible that says that infants should not be baptised.

In fact, in his famous sermon on Pentecost in Acts 2:38-39, Peter says: "Each one of you must turn away from his sins and be baptized in the name of Jesus Christ, so that your sins will be forgiven; and you will receive God's gift, the Holy Spirit. For God's promise was made to you and your children, and to all who are far away— all whom the Lord our God calls to himself." "Many of them believed his message and were baptized" (v.41), which include even infants and children.

What is Jesus' teaching about infant baptism?

According to Matthew 28:19, "Every man must be baptized" and is to be saved. Here Jesus does not make any distinctions between adult and children. And in Matthew 18:14, Jesus says "Father in heaven does not want any of these little ones to be lost." And further in the Gospel of John 3:5, Jesus says, "Truly, I say unto thee, except a man is born of water and of the Spirit, he cannot enter into the kingdom of God." The statement is universally applicable: unless A MAN is born again of water and the Spirit. So, Jesus says unless a man is born again of water and the Spirit he cannot enter into the Kingdom of God. Every man necessarily includes infants. It logically follows from the teaching of Jesus in John 3:5 that infants should be baptised.

"Then were there brought unto him little children that he should put his hands on them, and pray: and the disciples rebuked them. But Jesus said, 'Suffer little children, and forbid them not, to come unto me: for of such is the kingdom of heaven.' And he laid his hands on them, and departed thence" (Matt. 19:13-15). So Jesus makes clear to avail baptism and sanctifying grace to all children.

"To all people everywhere" clearly shows that Jesus wants everybody to become his disciples (Matt. 28:19).

What do the early Church Fathers say about infant baptism?

The early Church Fathers also believed in infant baptism, having received this tradition from Jesus and the Apostles (Catechism of Catholic Church, 1252). The biblical passages given below clearly show that the early Church Fathers believed in infant baptism.

"In the Church, baptism is given for the remission of sins, and, according to the usage of the Church, baptism is given even to infants. If there were nothing in infants which required the remission of sins and nothing in them pertinent to forgiveness, the grace of baptism would seem superfluous" (Origen, *Homilies on Leviticus* 8:3, 244-248 A.D.).

(Pope St. Innocent, 414 A.D) "Your Fraternity asserts the Pelagians preach, that even without the grace of Baptism infants are able to be endowed with the rewards of eternal life, is quite idiotic." (Jurgens, *The Faith of the Early Fathers*, Vol. 3: 2016).

St. Augustine, Letter to Jerome, 415 A.D: "Anyone who would say that even infants who pass from this life without participation in the Sacrament [of Baptism] shall be made alive in Christ truly goes counter to the preaching of the Apostle and condemns the whole Church, where there is great haste in baptizing infants because it is believed without doubt that there is no other way at all in which they can be made alive in Christ" (Jurgens, *The Faith of the Early Fathers*, Vol. 3:1439).

Martin Luther says God cannot allow children continue to live in the state of sin. Besides, major denominations like the Anglicans, the Episcopalians, the

Methodists, the Presbyterians and the Orthodox have the custom of giving infant baptism.

In the Catacombs, grave inscriptions also give proof of infant baptism: "Arckilla, age one and half, newly baptized girl, died on Feb. 23."

Why are children baptised? Is it not enough to baptise them after they grow up—because Jesus received baptism at the age of thirty?

No. It is not enough. Jesus received baptism at the age of thirty, but he said, "Let the children come to me and do not stop them, because the kingdom of God belongs to such as these" (Luke 18:15-16). So who are we to stop children or infants from coming to Jesus? Therefore, it is the will of God and the mother church that every child be baptised soon after birth (preferably on the eighth day after the birth for the male child and sixteenth day for the girl child). "The time came for Joseph and Mary to perform the ceremony of purification, as the Law of Moses commanded. So they took the child to Jerusalem to present him to the Lord" (Luke 2:22-24). Jesus received baptism at the age of thirty only for the fulfillment of the righteousness not for salvation or cleansing of the sins (Acts 16:3-15). Whereas in the matter of we the human (1Timothy 2:4-6) "the God our Savior wants everyone to be saved and to come to know the Truth. For there is one

God, and there is one who brings God and mankind together, the man Christ Jesus who gave himself to redeem all mankind. That was the proof at the right time that God wants everyone to be saved." So this is the will of God that every child born in this world be the child of His as soon as possible through receiving the Sacrament of Baptism. If the Sacrament of Baptism is the means of cleansing the Original Sin and receiving the Holy Spirit and consequently receiving the grace, why should we delay giving baptism to children? (Acts.2:38).

Many denominations (Protestants) do not accept infant baptism. They think baptism should be given only to those who have reached the age of reason and have chosen to receive it. They consider baptism of infants as invalid and unscriptural. However, for practical reasons, a number of denominations do give infant baptism, such as the Lutherans, the Anglicans, the Congregationalists, the Methodists, the Presbyterians, the CNI (*Uther Bharath Ki Kalisia Ki Aradhana Pusthak*, pp. 335-338) and others. Even Luther, who said that believing the Bible alone was enough for salvation, strongly believed in infant baptism.

Why do parents take the responsibility for giving baptism to children?

Parents are the instruments for giving birth to every child or bring life on to this earth. So also it is the responsibility of every parent to be the instrument for giving spiritual life. We know that children are innocent; they do not understand the value of knowledge and reason. So, why are they sent to school at such an innocent age? Why don't parents wait for the child to grow to the right age of reason and knowledge, when the child can decide for itself whether it should go to school or not? Why do parents dress the child? Why can't they wait for the child to grow so that it can decide whether it needs clothes or not? Just like the parents care for the child's future in this world, so also Catholic parents and the Church care for the spiritual welfare of the child. The parents know that Jesus is the Truth, Light and Way and Life for them as well as their children. So, it is the wish of every parent that their child be born as a Child of God and live in Christ.

Secondly, it is through parents that children come into the stain of sin. It is, therefore, the responsibility of parents to get salvation for their children too. This held good in the days of Jesus as well: "Salvation has come to this house today" (Luke 19:9), thus Zacchaeus became a source of salvation to all family members. He and all his family were baptized at once" (Acts 16:29-34). In Mark 5:22-43, we see Jesus giving life to Jairus' daughter at the request of him; and in Mark 9:17-27, at the request of a man, He heals his son from the evil spirit. Jesus himself said in Mark 16:16: "Whoever believes and is baptized will be saved; whoever does not believe will be condemned." Surely, parents do not wish their children to be condemned but saved. St. Peter says in Acts 2:38-39: "For God's promise was made to you and your children."

Is it enough to give baptism only to children?

No. We need to nurture them to grow in faith and teach them how to pray, accept Jesus as Lord and Saviour and the doctrines. In Ephesians 6:4, St. Paul says, "Bring them up with Christian discipline and instruction." According to Proverbs 19:18, "Discipline your children while they are young enough to learn. If you don't, you are helping them to destroy themselves." In 2 Maccabees, chapter 7, the mother's teaching gives courage to the seven children to die for their faith.

Why should children be baptised? Have they committed any sin?

This question was raised in the 4th century by Noastisists. According to them, children are not born of the Original Sin. In the 5th century, Pelagians said that Jesus died for all and his death sanctified all. Therefore, there is no need of baptism. The Church teaches that God created man in Holiness (Gen.1:27). But the first parents (Adam and

Eve) were wounded with the sin committed by them and the children born to them were born of the stain of this sin. St. Paul said in Rom. 5:12: "Sin came into the world through one man and his sin brought death with it. As a result, death has spread to the whole human race because everyone has sinned" (Rom.5:18-21). So, if baptism is compulsory for adults, it is necessary for infants too.

What about the children who have died without getting baptised?

As regards children who have died without baptism, the Church can only entrust them to the mercy of God. In Mark 10:14, Jesus says, "Let the children come to me, do not hinder them, because the kingdom of God belongs to such as these." It has become clearer that God wills that all men should attain eternal blessedness. This certainly includes children, who are seen in the gospels as the special objects of God's love. Secondly, that Christ was born and died for all. So, in view of these truths, there must be a way by which unbaptised infants are saved (A New Catechism, Catholic Faith for Adults, by Herder, N.Y., 1969).

CHAPTER **7**

Types of Baptism

In this chapter, we will look at the various types of baptism—the ways and means of administering baptism.

How many types of administration of baptism are there?

We must note that in the early Church, three types of baptism were in practice: immersion, pouring and sprinkling of water.

(1) Immersion: Lydia and her household were baptised by Paul in the river in Philippi (Acts 16:11-15).

(2) Pouring: In the Dedache, the disciples have written that the water is to be poured on the

head thrice invoking the baptismal form: "I will pour out my spirit on your children" (Isaiah 44:3).

(3)   Sprinkling of water: Water is a means of cleansing: "I will sprinkle clean water on you and make you clean from all your idols and everything else that has defiled you" (Ezek. 36:25).

Different types of baptism

- Baptism for the dead (1 Cor. 15:29)

- "By Moses in the cloud and in the sea" (1 Cor. 10)

- "Jesus said to them, 'Can you drink the cup that I must drink or be baptized with the baptism with which I must be baptized?' They replied, 'We can.' Jesus said to them, 'The cup that I must drink you shall drink, and with the baptism with which I must be baptized you shall be baptized'" (Mark 10:38-39). It denotes the suffering and death of Jesus and the martyrdom of his disciple; it symbolises the baptism of blood.

What is baptism of the dead?

Baptism is necessary to enter the Kingdom of God; therefore, everyone must have the opportunity to be baptised, including those who have died. Our Heavenly Father has provided a way that all may have the opportunity to accept or reject the gospel of Christ and be baptised.

Everyone born on earth will have the opportunity, whether in this life or in the next, to accept or reject the gospel of Jesus Christ and keep His commandments. In the Spirit World, the gospel is taught to the dead—to those who did not learn of it while living on earth. Apostle Peter taught the following principle in the Bible: "For this cause was the gospel preached also to them that are dead, that they might be judged according to men in the flesh, but live according to God in the spirit"(1 Peter 4:6). Apostle Paul also taught about baptism for the dead: "Else what shall they do which are baptized for the dead, if the dead rise not at all? Why are they then baptized for the dead?" (1 Cor. 15:29). We read in 2 Maccabees 12:43-45 of a sacrifice being offered for the sins of soldiers killed in battle, who were awaiting the resurrection. Also gives us an idea of baptism of the dead.

Jesus says, "I have a baptism to receive" (Luke 12:50). What does it mean? Why another baptism?

"I have a baptism to receive and how distressed I am until it is over!" (Luke 12:50) Jesus was speaking about his own sacrifice on the cross for the humanity—the real atonement he is supposed to achieve through his suffering, shedding of his blood, sacrifice on the cross and victory over evil, death and Satan through his resurrection.

What is the meaning of baptism of the Holy Spirit and fire (Luke 3:16)?

"Then they saw what looked like tongues of fire which spread out and touched each person there" (Acts 2.3). Here fire symbolises the energy and power of courage one receives. In

Luke 3.9, "Every tree that does not bear good fruit will be cut down and thrown in the fire."

"He will burn the chaff in a fire that never goes out" (Matt. 3.12). It also denotes the action of purifying, emptying and detachment.

"Put on sackcloth, and sat down in ashes" (Jonah 3.6). The ash symbolises change of life and acceptance of a new life. So fire stands for new life in Jesus.

What is the difference between John's baptism and Jesus' baptism?

There are many differences:

- In Luke 3:11, John the Baptist says, "I baptize you with water to show that you have repented, but the one who will come after me will baptize you with the Holy Spirit and fire." Therefore, it is clear that John used water to show one's repentance, whereas real baptism is reception of the Holy Spirit and fire— that is given only by Jesus to those who believe in him (Matt. 3:11, Acts 2:3-4; 2:38-39; 19:1-7).

- "All people went out to him confessing their sins and they were baptized by him in the Jordan River" (Mark 1:4). John's baptism is an invitation to repentance of one's sins (the word "sin" is plural). John the Baptist's baptism is baptism of self-repentance and it does not assure forgiveness; also, it does not give the Holy Spirit (Acts 19:1-7).

- "I came baptizing with water in order to make him known to the people of Israel" (John 1:31). "The baptism of John was for those who turned from their sins and he told the people of Israel to believe in the one who was coming after him" (Acts 19:4).

- John's baptism requires repentance and water but Jesus' baptism requires faith and the Holy Spirit, and then water (John 1:31-33). (Mark 1:5; John.3:23: He is the one who baptises with the Holy Spirit. If the sinner repents and confesses and turns away from the sins, then God will forgive); Jesus' baptism does assure forgiveness for all the sins and gives the Holy Spirit (Acts 19:1-6). He will baptise you with the Holy Spirit and fire (Acts 13:22-26).

- Whereas Jesus came to take away the affect of first parents' sin ('sin' is singular). "Here is the Lamb of God who takes away the sin of the world" (John 1:29). Peter replied, "Repent and be baptized every one of you in the name of Jesus Christ so that your sin may be forgiven and you will receive the Holy Spirit (Acts 2:38-39). "This is what you have heard from me; for John baptized with water, but you will be baptized with the Holy Spirit not many days from now" (Acts 1:4-5).

- It should be pointed out that in Catholic theology, the baptism given by John the Baptist was not the same as the baptism that Jesus instituted: the true Sacrament of Baptism. It did not have the same force or power.

- The baptism instituted by Jesus takes away the original and actual sins, as well as all the punishment due to sin; the baptism of John was a baptism that stirred people to repentance and was a pre-figuration of the baptism that Jesus instituted. That is why those who had only received the baptism of John were baptised again (Acts 19:4-5).

• John the Baptist's baptism does not have any of the Trinitarian forms. We use the Trinitarian form because it is a sacrament of communion with Almighty God fulfilled in the sanctifying action of Christ.

What kind of baptism did the disciples receive? From whom and when?

Most probably Jesus must have given the baptism to his disciples. "Jesus and his disciples went to the province of Judea, where he spent some time with them and baptized" (John 3:22, 26). "So they went to John and said, 'Teacher, you remember the man who was with you on the east side of the Jordan, the one you spoke about? Well he is baptizing now and everyone is going to him'" (v.26). Secondly, Jesus himself said to his disciples in John 15:3, "You have been made clean already by the teaching I have given you." And in John 13:8-11, v.10, Jesus says, "Anyone who had a bath is completely clean and does not have to wash himself, except for his feet." The very purpose of baptism is forgiveness of sin and reception of the Holy Spirit. So also the disciples were anointed by the Holy Spirit. John's Gospel reads: "Then he breathed on them and said, 'Receive the Holy Spirit' (John 20:22, 14:15-20). John the Baptist said, "The one who will come after me will baptize you with the Holy Spirit and fire" (Matt. 3:11). So after the death of Jesus anointed (baptized). "They saw what looked like tongues of fire which spread out and touched each person there. They were all filled with the Holy Spirit and began to talk in other languages" (Acts 2:3-4). Besides, we know the disciples were from the tribes of Jacob and as Jews they had undergone the ritual of purification (circumcision).

What kind of baptism did the people of the Old Testament have?

Since the beginning of the world, water, so humble and wonderful a creature, has been the source of life and fruitfulness. The sacred Scripture sees it as "overshadowed" by the Spirit of God (Gen. 1:2). The Church has seen in Noah's ark prefiguring of salvation by baptism, for by it a few, that is , eight persons, were saved through water" (1 Peter 3:20). The crossing of the Red Sea, literally the liberation of Israel from the slavery of Egypt, announces the liberation wrought by Baptism (Catechism of Catholic Church1239-1221, p.240). Just as no one escaped physical death at the hands of the Egyptians without crossing through the waters of the Red Sea, no one escapes eternal death without receiving the baptismal waters. Therefore, St. Paul says in 1 Corinthians 10:1-5, "Our ancestors were all under the cloud and all passed through the sea and all were baptized into Moses in the cloud and in the sea. And all ate the same spiritual food and all drank the same spiritual drink. For they drank from the spiritual rock that followed them, and the rock of Christ." And in Colossians 2:9, 13: "For in him the whole fullness of deity dwells bodily, and you have come to the fullness in him, who is the head of every ruler and authority. In him also you were circumcised with a spiritual circumcision, by putting off the body of the flesh in the circumcision of Christ; when you were buried with him in baptism, you also raised with him through faith in the power of God, who raised him from the dead. And when you were dead in trespasses and the un-circumcision of your flesh, God made you alive together with him, when he forgave us all our trespasses, erasing the record that stood against us with its legal demands" (v.13).

Some people object to this point. They bring up the good thief on the Cross (Luke 23:39-43) as an example against the necessity of baptism. But this example fails. First, the law of baptism, which Jesus made, binding on every man, became an obligation after Jesus' Resurrection, when Jesus gave the command to preach the Gospel and to baptise all nations in Matthew 28:20. The good thief died under the Old Law, before the Law of Baptism became binding on everyone. Secondly, the good thief did not go to Heaven on the very day that Jesus was crucified, because no one went to Heaven until after Jesus

did. Jesus had the primacy in all things, as St. Paul says
in Colossians 1:18. Jesus did not ascend into heaven until
after His Resurrection, as John 20:17 proves. So the good
thief is not an example against the necessity of baptism
for salvation. That is why the Nicene Creed correctly
states that Jesus was crucified, died and was buried;
He descended into Hell; on the third day, He rose again
from the dead and then ascended into Heaven. He did
not ascend to Heaven until after His Resurrection, and
He descended into Hell on the day of His death. What
was this Hell? It was Abraham's bosom, the waiting place
of the just of the Old Testament. That is where the good
thief went with Jesus on the day of His Crucifixion; Jesus
called it paradise because He would be there.

**Jesus said to one of the criminals on the cross, "I
promise you that today you will be in Paradise with
me" (Luke 23:43). How is it possible without
receiving baptism?**

Of course, baptism is a must to enter the kingdom of
heaven; but in the case of the criminal, faith in Jesus and
total repentance made his entry into heaven possible
without baptism. If he had time, probably he would have
received baptism too. In other words, the criminal was in
the state of reception of the baptism of faith. Jesus
himself said, "Happy are those who know they are

spiritually poor; the kingdom of heaven belongs to them" (Matt. 5:3). Therefore, Jesus said to Zacchaeus as well, "Salvation has come to this house today, for this man also is a descendant of Abraham" (Luke.19:9). Secondly, faith in Jesus saves us because he is the only one who died for our atonement.

What about people who die without baptism?

According to the scripture and the Christian faith, salvation is not possible without baptism. However, from the scripture we know that there are three types of baptism:

1. Baptism of Water—This is the common baptism; "they confessed their sins, and he baptized them in the River Jordan" (Matt. 3:5, 6).

2. Baptism of Blood—Martyrs; the killing of the innocent children (Matt. 2:16-18).

3. Baptism of Desire

   - Living in good conscience. "If you confess that Jesus is Lord and believe that God raised him from death, you will be saved" (Rom. 10:9).

   - Due to situation, the good thief was saved (Luke 23:43), where we see the repented thief has been rewarded by Jesus with the promise that the thief would be in the kingdom of God.

- In spite of the intention of the parents and the Church the child who dies without baptism is also saved.

So from above points we can conclude that without the reception of Baptism of water one would also be saved at least through the baptism of blood or desire.

CHAPTER 8

Circumcision and Baptism

Why did Jesus and every Jewish child undergo the ritual of circumcision?

Because we learn from Luke 2:23; Jesus was presented in the Temple on the eighth day; it was not just a ritual but a sign of God's Covenant to his children (Gen. 17:1-14; Lev. 12:1-7). Baptism is not a ritual but a Sacrament.

Is the purpose of the Old Testament circumcision the same as that of the New Testament baptism?

There is no doubt that circumcision was the Old Testament counterpart of baptism. Letter to Colossians, chapter 2, teaches that baptism is the New Testament circumcision. Circumcision was the way through which males in the Old Testament entered a covenantal relationship with God. If you were not circumcised, you were not in God's covenant. Colossians 2:11-12 says: "In [Jesus] also you are circumcised with the circumcision made without hands, in putting off the body of the sins of the flesh by the circumcision of Christ: Buried with him in baptism, wherein also ye are risen with him through the faith…" This passage identifies baptism as the new and greater circumcision. It also says that one rises to new supernatural life in Christ by baptism.

CHAPTER 9

Frequently Asked Questions about Baptism

This chapter addresses a number of questions frequently asked with regard to baptism, such as God Parents, authorised persons to administer baptism and sin after baptism.

How many times can we receive baptism?

We can receive baptism only once, because Jesus died once and for all and for all ages; therefore, there is only one baptism.

"There is one body and one Spirit, just as you were called to the one hope of your calling. One Lord, One faith, One Baptism, One God and One Father of all, who is above all and through all and in all" (Eph. 4:4-6).

Therefore, if we receive more than once, we are going against the Word of God. Romans 6:1-14 says, "For whoever has died is freed from sin. But we have died with Christ; we will also live with him. We know that Christ, being raised from the dead, will never die again: death no longer has dominion over him.... The death he died, he died to sin, once for all; but the life he lives, he lives to God."

There is no circumcision the second time. So also we cannot have the true baptism more than once. Romans 2:25: "Circumcision indeed is of value if you obey the law but if you break the law, your circumcision has become uncircumcision." But then we must know that we cannot have circumcision repeatedly.

Why do we pour water thrice?

1. To symbolise the Trinitarian aspect.

2. To symbolise Jesus' three-day presence in the grave.

3. To symbolise his suffering, death and burial and resurrection.

Who is (are) authorised to administer the sacrament of baptism?

There were many disciples and followers of Christ (Luke.10:1-12; John.19:25-26) but he did not give them the power to baptise; except to the eleven disciples. And from Matthew 28:16-20, we know that only "the eleven disciples went to the hill in Galilee where Jesus had told them to go. Jesus drew near and said to them: "I have been given all authority in heaven and on earth. Go then to all peoples everywhere and make them my disciples; baptise them in the name of the Father, the Son and the Spirit and teach them to obey everything I have commanded you." Even St. Paul who claimed to be the disciple apologised that he was not appointed to give baptism but to preach. Therefore, he did not give Baptism except only to a few. "I thank God that I did not baptize any of you except Crispus and Gaius, and Stephanus and his family; but I can't remember whether I baptized anyone else. For Christ did not send me to baptize but to proclaim the gospel" (1 Cor. 1:14, 16-17).

Why suffering and illnesses continue to stay with us even after baptism?

"Certain temporal consequences of sin remain in the baptized, such as suffering, illness, death, and such frailties in life as weakness of character, and so on, as well as an inclination to sin that tradition calls concupiscence, or tinder for sin. This is for us to wrestle with, it cannot harm those who do not consent but manfully resist it by the grace of Jesus Christ" (Council of Trent). Indeed, "an athlete is not crowned unless he competes according to the rules" (2 Tim. 2:5; Rom. 9:19-26; 1 Pet. 1:6-7; 2:20-24; 3:16-19; 4:12-19).

Is baptism alone enough for salvation?

No. We receive the sanctifying grace in baptism. It can be lost if we are not living a life that is spiritual according to the scriptures (Eph. 1:2-14). Besides, we need to pray tirelessly and receive other sacraments too, especially reception of the Holy Communion. According to John 6:53-58, v.54, "Whoever eats my flesh and drinks my blood has eternal life, and I will raise him to life on the last day."

Only the person who is put right with God through faith shall live (Gal. 3:11). Is it true?

Yes. But Paul answers by quoting from Lev.18.5. Gal. 3:12 says that "whoever does everything the law requires will live." Also, in James 2:14-18, it is said that "good works without faith is useless; faith without good works also useless." Therefore, faith and good works go hand in hand. In Matthew.7:21-23, Jesus says, "Not everyone who calls me 'Lord, Lord' will enter the kingdom of heaven, but only those who do what my Father in heaven wants them to do. When the Judgment day comes, many will say to me, 'Lord, Lord! In your name we spoke God's message, by your name we drove out many demons and performed many miracles!' then I will say to them, 'I never knew you. Get away from me, you wicked people!'"

When should we give baptism to a new member?

When one is ready; it means that one may be given baptism when the church feels that one has come to total faith in communion with the Church, grown spiritually, matured and shown the readiness to receive baptism.

Why are the newly baptised given a Christian name?

As a sign of new life in Jesus Christ (Acts chapters 9 and 22—Saul is called Paul; Matthew 16:16-18—where Simon, son of John, is called as Peter) and to imitate the person whose name they bear.

Why God Parents?

Baptism is the sacrament of faith, and one receives faith through the community of believers. And even after baptism, a new recipient needs to be continually nurtured in faith. Therefore, there should be god parents who are firm believers, able and ready to help the newly baptised on the road of Christian life. Their task is a truly ecclesial function. The whole ecclesial community bears some responsibility for the development and safeguarding of the grace given at baptism (Mark.2:3-5; Mark.6:55-56; Luke.9:37-43).

Can we use any liquid for baptism?

No. There are many liquids available for cleansing and drinking (petrol, spirit and saline), but it does not mean that we use all of them for drinking and taking bath. So also, according to the Holy Bible, other than simple water, no other liquid is to be used for baptism.

What is the Sacrament of Confirmation?

The Sacrament of Confirmation is the confirmation of faith and reception of the Holy Spirit knowingly and willingly. This is the second step after baptism. For example, Luke 24:50, 51: "Then he led them out of the city as far as Bethany, where he raised his hands and blessed them. As he was blessing them, he departed from them and was taken up into heaven."

"When the day of Pentecost came, all the believers were gathered together in one place. Suddenly there was a noise from the sky which sounded like a strong wind blowing and it filled the whole house where they were sitting. Then they saw what looking like tongues of fire which spread out and touched each person there. They were all filled with the Holy Spirit and began to talk other languages, as the spirit enabled them to speak. Do not leave Jerusalem but wait for the gift I told you about the gift my Father promised. John baptized with water, but

in a few days you will be baptized with the Holy Spirit"
(Acts 2:1-5). "But when the Holy Spirit comes upon
you, you will be filled with power and you will be witnesses
for me" (v. 8). "They sent Peter and John to them and
they went down, and prayed for the Samaritans to receive
the Holy Spirit, for as yet he had not come down on any
of them: they had only been baptized in the name of the
Lord Jesus; they laid hands on them, and they received
the Holy Spirit" (Acts 8:14-17).

Why was John baptising in the wilderness?

"John was baptizing in Aenon near Salim because there
was much water there" (John 3:23).

Why was it necessary for Jesus to be baptised by John in the river Jordan?

The baptism of repentance was a custom of the Jews
and so it was not compulsory for Jesus "that you have
repented" (Matt. 3:11). So the passage continues saying
in Matthew 3:13-15 that Jesus arrived from Galilee and
came to John at the Jordan river to be baptised by him.
But John tried to make him change his mind saying, "I
ought to be baptized by you…and yet you have come to
me." But Jesus answered him, "Let it be so now for it is
proper for us in this way to fulfill all righteousness."

Secondly, Jesus submitted to baptism to show all men that it is necessary to be baptised. Baptism is so necessary that even Jesus who was both true God and true man submitted himself to it. He was baptised by John the Baptist to show that every single man must be baptised for one's own salvation. Jesus' reception of baptism at the hands of John is considered to be the transition between John's prefigured baptism and the real baptism of Christ. The baptism of Jesus sanctified the waters so that they could be efficacious in taking away sin, even though the baptism that Jesus would institute would not become binding on all until after the resurrection.

Thirdly, "Jesus did not receive baptism as a confession of guilt on His own account. He identified Himself with sinners, taking the steps that we are to take and doing the work that we must do. His life of suffering and patient endurance after His baptism was also an example to us" (E. G. White, *Desire of Ages*, pg.111).

What is the importance of Jesus' baptism?

- His simplicity and humility (Matt. 3:14).

- Revealing himself to John the Baptist (John 1:30-34).

- Becoming one with humanity (Eph. 2:14-22).

Did Jesus give baptism to anybody?

"Jesus and his disciples went to the province of Judea where he spent some time with them and baptized" (John 3:22). "So they went to John and said 'Teacher you remember the man who was with you on the east side of the Jordan, the one you spoke about? Well, he is baptizing now and everyone is going to him'" (v.26).

When we look at John 4:1, 2, we find that Jesus was not baptising anybody. "The Pharisees heard that Jesus was winning and baptizing more disciples than John. Actually, Jesus himself did not baptize anyone, only his disciples did."

Is it true that when one receives baptism, one experiences the strong wind blowing, receives spirit in tongues of fire and speaks in other languages?

"Suddenly there was a noise from the sky which sounded like a strong wind blowing, and it filled the whole house where they were sitting. Then they saw what looked like tongues of fire which spread out and touched each person there. They were all filled with the Holy Spirit and began to talk in other languages, as the spirit enabled them to speak" (Acts 2:2-4).

This is the only incident where they had these experiences by receiving the Holy Spirit. Whereas in the same chapter (Acts 2:40-42), we see St. Peter preaching and giving baptism to about 3,000 people. But none of them could experience and speak in different languages as it is mentioned in (Acts 2:2-4).

While receiving baptism from John the Baptist, Jesus or others did not speak in any other language than what they knew; instead Jesus had some other experiences in Mark 1:10-11. Therefore, it is not necessary that all those who receive baptism should experience the wind, see the tongues of fire and speak in other languages.

CHAPTER 10

Baptism and Salvation

Every person who believes in God believes in salvation or life after death. According to Scripture, those born of flesh and blood need salvation. Salvation is possible only through Jesus and baptism.

Why is baptism compulsory for every human?
According to John 3:3-8, "I am telling you the truth no one can see the kingdom of God unless he is born again" (v 3). "No one can enter the kingdom of God unless he is born of water and the Spirit, born spiritually of the Spirit, born again means born of the Holy Spirit"(v.5). Jesus said to his eleven Apostles in Mark 16:16 "whoever believes and is baptized will be saved whoever does not believe will be condemned." (The beliefs of Hinduism, that is, Death and Rebirth; in other words, one is caught

up in the circle of 84,00,000 Yug chakra, due to which one loses eternal life. This eternal life could be attained by ritual practice of dipping oneself in the river Ganges while one is alive or after death. Only by breaking the chakra can one attain Moksha or salvation or eternal life.)

Every human is the victim of the Original Sin and rebirth. All are looking for salvation (Eternal life or Bliss, *Amrith Jeevan, Moksha, Mukthi, Sachkhand*). But one is not able to get it by himself or herself. Therefore, one is needed to depend on someone else, who is Jesus Himself. So, St. Paul says in Romans 5:12-19, "Sin came into the world through one man, and his sin brought death with it. As a result, death has spread to the whole human race because everyone has sinned. It is true that many people died because of the sin of that one man. But God's grace is much greater; so is the grace of one man, Jesus Christ. As one sin condemned all mankind, in the same way, the one righteous act sets all mankind free and gives them life. And just as all people were made sinners as the result of the disobedience of one man, in the same way they will all be put right with God as the result of the obedience of the one man." And in Galatians 3:25-29, we read as "for in Christ Jesus you are all children of God through faith. As many of you as were baptized in Christ have clothed yourselves with Christ. (Rev.7:8-9, 13-14: only those in white robes are in the kingdom of heaven). There is no longer Jew or Greek, there is no longer slave or free, there is no longer male or female; for all of you belong to Christ, then you are Abraham's offspring, heirs according to the promise."

Again, in Romans 6:2-7, he says "We have died to sin. For surely when we were baptized into union with Christ Jesus, we were baptized into union with his death. By our Baptism then we were buried with him and shared his death, in order that just as Christ was raised from death by the glorious power of the Father, so also we may live a new life." And in 1 Corinthians 15:21-22, "For just as death came by means of a man in the same way the rising from death comes by means of a man. For just as all people die because of their union with Adam, in the same way all will be raised to life because of their union with Christ."

What are the graces that follow the one who believes in Jesus?

The graces that follow the one who believes in Jesus are according to John 7:38-39 "streams of life giving water will pour out from his heart. Jesus said this about the Spirit which will be received by those who believe in him." And according to Mark 16:17-18, "believers will be given the power to perform miracles, they will drive out demons in my name; they will speak in strange tongue, if they pick up snakes or drink any poison, they will not be harmed they will place their hands on sick people, who will get well."

Did Jesus bring salvation to all?

Yes. But in John 3:36, it is said, "whoever believes in the Son has eternal life; whoever disobeys the Son will not have life; but will remain under God's punishment." "That is why I told you that you will die in your sins if you do not believe that 'I Am Who I Am'" (John 8:24). "You may believe that Jesus is the Christ the son of God, and that believing this you may have life through his name" (John 20:31).

Jesus teaches that all men must have faith and be baptised and saved. Because no one can be saved without it, as we see in Mark 16:15-16: "And he (Jesus) said to them: Go through out whole world and preach the Gospel to all mankind. Whoever believes and is baptized will be saved; whoever does not believe will be condemned." "And Jesus came and spoke unto them, saying, all power is given unto me in heaven and in earth. Go you therefore, and teach all nations, baptizing them in the name of the Father, and of the Son, and of the Holy Spirit: Teaching them to observe all things whatsoever I have commanded you…" (Matt. 28:18-20). Jesus says that those who believe and are baptized will be saved, which indicates that the un-baptised will not be saved. But some ask why Jesus did not say that "He that believeth not and is not baptized shall be damned," after saying he that believeth and is baptized shall be saved? The answer is that those who do not believe are not going to get baptized, so it is not necessary to mention baptism again. "In the same manner Christ also was offered in sacrifice once to take away the sins of many. He will appear a second time not to deal with sin but to save those who are waiting for him" (Heb. 9:28).

By believing in Jesus' salvific action, which is objective and by receiving baptism, one subjectively takes part in this salvific action of Jesus, which took place 2000 years ago at Jerusalem. The Bible says that disobedience of the first parents became the cause of losing eternal life (*Amrit Jeevan*). Since then this was a constant effort for human to achieve the kingdom of God (lost world or *Sachkhand*, *Swarg*). This constant trial never became successful until it could happen in Jesus who shed his Sacrificial Pure Blood on Calvary. Jesus' blood bypassed all the other blood that was offered in human history. Because the other blood offered was impure.

What are the things required for salvation?

First, true baptism: "Jesus answered and said unto him, Truly, truly, I say unto thee, except a man be born again, he cannot see the kingdom of God. Nicodemus said to him, how can a man be born when he is old? Can he enter the second time into his mother's womb, and be born? Jesus answered, Truly, Truly, I say unto thee, except a man be born of water and of the Spirit, he cannot enter into the kingdom of God" (John 3:3-5).

Secondly, Faith in Jesus and in his teaching: "Go therefore and make disciples of all nations, baptizing them in the name of the Father and of the Son and of the Holy Spirit, and teaching them to obey everything that I have commanded you" (Matt. 28:19-20). "Not everyone who calls me 'Lord, Lord' will enter the Kingdom of heaven, but only those who do what my father in heaven wants them to do" (Matt. 7:21).

Thirdly, observing His commandment: After Baptism one is expected to obey Jesus' Commandments or walk according to the Gospel. "I give you a new commandment that you love one another. Just as I have loved you, you also should love one another. By this everyone will know that you are my disciple, if you have love for one another" (John.13:34, 35). "Henceforth we should not serve sin" (Rom. 6:5).

Fourthly, Reception of the Body and Blood of Christ: "I am telling you the truth; if you do not eat the flesh of the Son of the Man and drink his blood, you will not have life in yourselves. Whoever eats my flesh and drinks my blood has eternal life, and I will raise him to life on the last day. For my flesh is the real food; my blood is the real drink" (John.6:53-55).

Fifth, Confession or Reconciliation: "Turn away from your sins." "If your brother sins, rebuke him and if he repents, forgive him" (Luke 17:3-4). "I tell you, there will be more joy in heaven over one sinner who repents than over ninety-nine respectable people who do not need to repent" (Luke 15:7). "I tell you, the angels of God rejoice over one sinner who repents" (Luke 15:10). "The prayer made in faith will heal the sick person... and the sins he committed will be forgiven. So then confess your sins to one another and pray for one another, so that you will be healed" (James 5:15). "But if we confess our sins to God he will keep his promise and do what is right: he will forgive us our sins and purify us from all our wrongdoing" (1 John 1:8-10). "If you forgive people's sins, they are forgiven; if you do not forgive them, they are not forgiven" (John 20:21-23).

Who will be in the Kingdom of heaven?

According to the signs given in the passage Revelation 7:1-17, refer to the Catholic Church. "Do not harm...until we mark the servants of our God with a seal on their foreheads. And the number of marked is 144,000" (Rev. 7:3, 4). "They are from twelve tribes" (vs. 5-8). "There was the Lamb standing on Mount Zion; with him were 144,000 people who have his name and his Father's name written on their foreheads" (Rev. 14:1-5). "They are the men who have kept themselves pure by not having sexual relations with women; they are virgins. They follow the lamb wherever he goes. They have been redeemed from the rest of mankind and are the first ones to be offered to God and to the Lamb" (v. 4). Therefore, it can be said that these anointed ones are the bishops of the Mother Church and those in union with the church.

"There was an enormous crowd—no one could count all the people! They were from every race, tribe, nation, and language, and they stood in front of the throne and of the Lamb, dressed in white robes and holding palm branches in their hands. They called out in a loud voice: 'Salvation comes from our God, who sits on the throne, and from the Lamb'" (Rev. 7:9-10). First and foremost, if looked at the number of Christians spread out throughout the whole universe, only Catholics can be seen;

other denominations are not found everywhere as the Catholics are. Secondly, it is only the Catholics who have the Tabernacle, the throne of the Lamb and Presence of the Holy Eucharist. Thirdly, again, it is mostly the Catholics who are traditionally dressed in white, especially on the reception of every sacrament, besides Sunday suit and holding Palm leaves and standing in praise of Jesus on Palm Sunday in front of the Tabernacle in the Church.

"These are the people who have come safely through the terrible persecution. They have washed their robes and made them white with the blood of the Lamb. That is why they stand before God's throne and serve him day and night in his temple. He who sits on the throne will protect them with his presence" (Rev. 7:14-15). I do not think that anyone other than the Catholics prays and adores in the Temple of God day and night in front of Blessed Sacrament (God's throne).

So from the above passage I am sure, it is the Catholics and those who are in union with this, will be found on the last day in the Kingdom of God.